What Was the Wild West?

What Was
the Wild West?

by Janet B. Pascal

illustrated by Stephen Marchesi

Penguin Workshop

For George and David, my Texas boys—JBP

For Alex—go west, young man,
at least for a visit—SM

PENGUIN WORKSHOP
An Imprint of Penguin Random House LLC, New York

Text copyright © 2017 by Janet B. Pascal.
Illustrations copyright © 2017 by Penguin Random House LLC. All rights reserved.
Published by Penguin Workshop, an imprint of Penguin Random House LLC, New York.
PENGUIN and PENGUIN WORKSHOP are trademarks of Penguin Books Ltd.
WHO HQ & Design is a registered trademark of Penguin Random House LLC.
Manufactured in China.

Visit us online at www.penguinrandomhouse.com.

Library of Congress Control Number: 2017941418

ISBN 9780399544248   10 9 8 7 6 5 4 3 2 1

Part of the *What Is America?* Boxed Set, ISBN 9780593089781

Contents

What Was the Wild West?

In 1886, crowds gathered in New York's Madison Square Garden to applaud one of the decade's biggest traveling shows—"Buffalo Bill's Wild West." The cast included real cowboys and hundreds of Native Americans. Over the course of two thrilling hours, the audience saw the story of "how the West was won."

Indians on horseback hunted live buffalo.

Bandits attacked an actual stagecoach. The famous sharpshooter Annie Oakley shot a cigar right out of her husband's mouth. Cowboys rode bucking broncos and roped cattle. In the end, a band of Indian warriors attacked a pioneer settlement and were soundly defeated.

Buffalo Bill Cody, who ran the show, was a genuine Wild West hero. As a teenager, he rode a horse across the prairie for the Pony Express mail service. He scouted in the Indian Wars. He earned his nickname by

BUFFALO BILL

killing 4,282 buffalo in eighteen months to feed workers who were building a railroad across the country.

Buffalo Bill's show was wildly popular. At the world's fair in Chicago in 1893, millions of people came to see it. When it toured Europe, England's Queen Victoria was a fan. The show was largely responsible for the popular legend of the Wild West that movies, TV shows, and novels still draw on. The real story of the western frontier, however, is much more complicated.

CHAPTER 1
The Frontier

So what—and where—was the Wild West?

To the Indian nations that had been living in North America for thousands of years, the West wasn't "wild." It was part of their home. From the Seminole in the Southeast to the Duwamish in the Northwest, there were many nations. Each

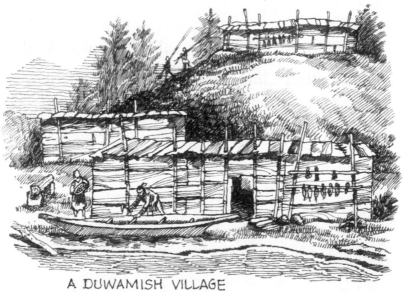

A DUWAMISH VILLAGE

had its own culture with distinct beliefs, languages, and lifestyles. The different tribes all believed in respecting the land they lived on. They didn't think that a single person could own a piece of land privately. A Wampanoag leader told some of the first settlers, "The land is our mother, nourishing all her children. . . . The woods, the streams, everything on it belongs to everybody and is for the use of all. How can one man say it belongs to him only?"

SOME OF THE
TRIBES IN THE EARLY 1700s

TLINGIT
CHIPEWYAN
NASKAPI
PUWAMISH
CREE
BLACKFOOT
PENOBSCOT
YAKIMA
SIOUX
OJIBWA
IROQUOIS
NEZ PERCE
CROW
HIDATSA
HURON
CHEYENNE
SAUK
FOX
WAMPANOAG
POMO
SHOSHONE
ARAPAHO
MIAMI
DELAWARE
PAIUTE
UTE
SHAWNEE
YOKUTS
KANSAS
POWHATTAN
NAVAJO
CHEROKEE
HOPI
OSAGE
PUEBLO
KIOWA
APACHE
CHICKASAW
PIMA
COMANCHE
CHOCTAW
CREEK
SEMINOLE
TAINO
COAHUILTECAN
ARAWAK

The American Indians didn't see the lands where they lived as wilderness. However, to the first white settlers from Europe, anywhere farther inland than the colonies along the Eastern Seaboard was wilderness—the "Wild West." It was untamed, and untouched by civilization. These settlers often lumped different native people together into one group. They considered them all savages.

Europeans thought land was meant to be owned, and that it was humankind's duty to tame nature and make the land useful—to grow crops, build towns. In the New World, they cut down forests, built roads, bridged rivers, and started farms. They brought their laws and religion to people they saw as uncivilized. As the population grew, people moved westward. A line—not a real one, but a line on a map— marked the border between settled territory and the land the colonists hadn't explored yet. That

line was called the frontier.

Native Americans saw the frontier as the line where a strange people challenged their ideas and values, and tried to force a new way of life on them. As the line moved farther and farther west, their civilization was pushed into a smaller and smaller space.

It's no wonder the frontier, where the two cultures met, was often a violent place.

CHAPTER 2
Log Cabin Pioneers

At the end of the eighteenth century, the line of the frontier ran through the ancient forests of the Appalachian Mountains.

In a treaty in 1763, the English government had promised the Indians all the land west of the mountains. The idea was that the English colonists would settle along the East Coast. Any Indians living there would move west, where they could live in their own way.

After the Revolutionary War, however, the population of the new United States of America grew. The country became hungry for more and more land to farm. So the government decided it was not bound by this treaty, since it had been made by another country—Great Britain.

NEW HAMPSHIRE
NEW YORK
MASSACHUSETTS
RHODE ISLAND
CONNECTICUT
PENNSYLVANIA
NEW JERSEY
DELAWARE
MARYLAND
VIRGINIA
NORTH CAROLINA
SOUTH CAROLINA
GEORGIA
MISSISSIPPI RIVER
OHIO RIVER
INDIAN RESERVE
WEST FLORIDA
EAST FLORIDA

MAP OF AMERICA IN 1763

In 1785, the government divided the land along the Ohio River valley into square plots and sold them to settlers. This would not be the last time Americans broke a treaty when they wanted the land for themselves.

Sometimes the Indians and the new settlers managed to live side by side. Many Indians were eager to trade for useful goods like guns and metal tools. As long as there was enough room, each group could live in its own fashion, without getting in each other's way.

As the farmland filled up, the cultures clashed

more often. With settlers demanding more and more land, Indians were forced to move farther west. However, some Indians attacked settlers who were taking over their hunting grounds. They burned cabins and killed or enslaved the people living there. To the US government, this just proved Indians were savages.

Building a Log Cabin

For the settlers, turning the ancient forest into a home was hard work. First they had to cut down huge trees. Then they dug up the stumps and cleared out the rocks to make a field to farm. They needed to build a place to live. There were no stores to buy building material, but there were lots of logs. So they built log cabins. This didn't even require nails. All they needed was an ax.

To build the cabin, a settler chopped a notch near each end of the logs. He fitted the notches into each other snugly so there wouldn't be any gaps. Then he filled in the chinks between the logs with mud. Most log cabins had one room. If there were windows, they were covered by shutters or animal skins, not glass.

Working alone, a man could build a log cabin in about a week. But it was much easier with a group of people. Neighbors from miles around would gather to help build and to enjoy one another's company.

The log cabin became a symbol for how Americans wanted to see themselves. Living in one showed you were brave, strong, and independent. Seven US presidents were born in log cabins. The most famous is Abraham Lincoln, who was born in a cabin in Kentucky in 1809.

While settlers were slowly clearing patches of forest, another group of men was ranging over the continent. These were the fur trappers, or "mountain men." Fur was one of the most valuable goods the New World had to sell abroad.

Beaver skins were in special demand. They were used to make the hats that everybody wore—especially gentlemen's tall top hats.

Mountain men were hired to go deep into the forests and trade with the Indians for furs. They depended on friendly Indians to help them survive. Most of them adopted Indian customs, and many of them married Indian women.

Starting in 1825, a giant fair called the Rendezvous (say: RON-day-voo) was held once a year out in the wilderness. Thousands of trappers, Indians, and traders gathered together for a month to buy and sell furs. One mountain man described the meeting as "mirth, songs, dancing, shouting, trading, running, jumping, singing, racing, target-shooting, yarns, frolic, with all sorts of extravagances that white men or Indians could

INDIANS AND TRAPPERS AT A RENDEZVOUS

invent." Then the trappers went back into the forests. Many of them didn't see settled land for years.

The mountain men became folk heroes. They told amazing stories of their adventures. One described how a grizzly bear took his whole head into its mouth. His scalp was torn off, but his friends sewed him back together. Then he went on as if nothing had happened. Another ran out of food. So he roasted his leather moccasins over the fire and ate them.

The beaver-fur trade boomed until about 1840. Then beaver hats went out of fashion. Many fur traders were out of work. Since they had spent so much time exploring the wilderness, they knew the land better than any other settlers. Many of them became useful as guides to people hoping to move farther west.

Daniel Boone (1734–1820)

Daniel Boone was the most legendary mountain man of all. In 1775 he discovered one of the few paths that crossed the Appalachian Mountains into Kentucky. Later he led people over it to start one of the first settlements west of the mountains. He became the hero of many tall tales. It was said that once, when he was attacked by a bear, he reached all the way down its throat, grabbed its tail, and yanked until he had turned the bear inside out.

DANIEL BOONE

CHAPTER 3
The Oregon Trail

Americans believed in something called "Manifest Destiny." They thought the United States was meant to stretch across the entire continent, from sea to shining sea. By the early 1840s, most good farmland as far as the Mississippi and Missouri Rivers was claimed.

People thought the prairie was too hard to farm. So they turned their attention to the Oregon Territory, thousands of miles away on the West Coast. They knew about this land from fur traders

--- OREGON TRAIL, THE ROUTE TAKEN TO THE WEST

and a few missionaries who had gone to convert the Indians. Wonderful stories were told about Oregon. The ground was so rich you could raise a crop without working. The climate was so mild no one ever got sick.

1843 was the year of what was called the Great Migration. About one thousand pioneers traveled to Oregon. They needed about 160 days to cross the prairie and reach the mountain ranges in the West. Travelers had to set out in early spring after the ground was dry. Otherwise their wagons would get stuck in the deep mud. And they had to cross the mountains before winter snows made it too dangerous.

Most pioneers used large wagons pulled by a team of oxen. They were called "prairie schooners," because their arched canvas covers made them look like ships sailing across the grassland.

They were packed so full, there was no room to sit. People chose what to pack very carefully. They needed enough supplies to survive the trip and to start a new life. Sometimes they also took a few precious treasures such as pianos, books, or china. Later, when travel got rough, they might have to abandon these things at the side of the trail to lighten their load.

Some travelers couldn't afford a wagon but were determined to go to Oregon anyway. One widow walked all the way to Oregon with her five children, the youngest of whom was only six. She hauled their possessions in a handcart.

Groups of pioneers banded together under a leader to form a wagon train. On the trail, they got up at five in the morning and traveled about twenty miles a day. In the evening the wagons formed a circle, each chained to the ones beside it. This made a barricade. Inside the circle, people could relax. They used buffalo droppings—called buffalo chips—to build fires. After dinner there was sometimes music and dancing.

During the night, an armed guard stood watch. Indians such as the Sioux, Shoshone, Kiowa, Crow, and Paiute lived along the trail. People were afraid they would attack. The wagon trains were traveling over the Indians' land.

The pioneers did not treat it respectfully. They cut down trees. Their cattle ate all the grass for miles around and destroyed the Indians' crops. Even so, Indian attacks were very rare.

CROW

PAIUTE

Still, crossing the plains was a hard, dangerous trip. The pioneers moved in a choking cloud of dust. There were swift rivers that the horses and cattle had to wade or swim across. Sometimes there were storms with wind so strong, the wagons had to be chained together so they wouldn't blow away.

It was hard to find clean drinking water. Pioneers got a sickness called cholera from polluted water. Someone could be healthy in the morning, and dead by nightfall. The Oregon Trail is lined with the unmarked graves of people who died along the way.

After the trail crossed the Rocky Mountains, the trip got even harder. The trail led through dry desert and rocky canyons. The worst part was crossing the Blue Mountains.

There was no good pass there. Sometimes the rocks were so steep that people had to take their wagons apart. They hauled their wagon and belongings up piece by piece, and then put the wagon back together.

On the other side of the pass, at the city of The Dalles, parties split off, depending on where they wanted to go. The official end of the Oregon Trail was Oregon City. By 1860, more than three hundred thousand pioneers had traveled the Oregon Trail. Their wagon wheels wore ruts so deep into the earth that, in some places, they are still there today.

OREGON CITY, 1860s

Independence Rock

Near where the trail crossed the Rocky Mountain pass stood Independence Rock, known as "the Great Register of the Desert." Here more than five thousand settlers carved their names and the date. When travelers got there, they searched the rock, hoping to find the names of friends and family who had gone before them. Some groups celebrated having gotten so far by holding a dancing party on the rock's flat top. Many pioneers' names can still be read today.

CHAPTER 4
Home on the Range

Another group also rode over the prairies without settling on them—the men who took charge of huge herds of cattle. These were the original cowboys. Later on, people started using the word *cowboy* for bandits, outlaws, thieves, and murderers—people who had nothing to do with cows. But the real cowboys worked hard and were honorable.

The land around Texas became part of the United States in 1845. Most of it was used for raising cattle. These were not gentle, friendly milk cows. They were huge steers with sharp horns. The most common type was the Texas longhorn, with horns as long as six feet, from tip to tip.

Ranchers didn't need to own fields. They raised free-range cattle. This means the steers were turned loose to wander wherever they wanted on the open range all year. They grazed on land that didn't belong to anyone.

Each steer had its owner's brand burned into its hide so it could be recognized. The brands had special names. A *P* lying on its side was called a "lazy P," and an *A* with wings would be a "flying A."

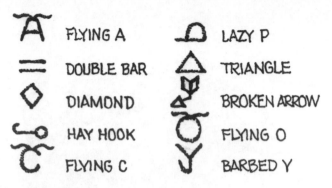

FLYING A		LAZY P	
DOUBLE BAR		TRIANGLE	
DIAMOND		BROKEN ARROW	
HAY HOOK		FLYING O	
FLYING C		BARBED Y	

Sometimes thieves called cattle rustlers stole cows. They would change the brands so it looked like the animals were theirs. For instance, a "flying C" could be turned into a "flying O" by closing up the circle. So ranchers had to think of clever brands that couldn't be changed. Cattle rustling was considered a terrible crime. If a rustler was caught, he might be killed on the spot.

Cowboys needed boots that were strong enough to be worn for many days while riding. A cowboy's hat had to be waterproof, with a broad brim to shield the wearer from fierce sun. They were called "ten-gallon hats." No one knows why for sure. Even the biggest hat could never hold ten gallons! Leather coverings over their pants, called chaps, protected their legs from being scratched by the bushes. Around their necks they wore bandannas to prevent sunburn. Sometimes they covered their mouths with the bandanna to keep themselves from breathing dust.

TEN-GALLON HAT

BANDANNA

CHAPS

Cowboys used a looped rope called a lasso to grab steers and to capture wild horses called broncos. Training these horses took courage. Few men could stay on the back of

a bucking bronco for long. Cowboys sometimes got together to compete with one another and show off their skills in roping and riding. These gatherings grew into shows called rodeos.

Some cowboys became famous for their courage or their crazy stunts. The half-black, half-Indian Bill Pickett was known for "bull-dogging." When he wanted to capture a steer, he would jump off his horse, grab the steer by the horns, and bite its lip.

BILL PICKETT

Black, white, Indian, and Hispanic cowboys all worked together. On the ranch they lived together in a large bunkhouse. Every spring, they rounded up the herds and drove them to market.

At first, this wasn't a long trip. Ranchers sold their cattle in nearby towns. But by the 1860s, train lines were beginning to stretch out from the East

Coast cities to new "cow towns" on the edge of
the prairie. Ranchers could sell their cattle for
more money in these towns—places like Wichita
or Abilene in Kansas. Then the meat was shipped
back east. Soon herds were being driven hundreds
of miles north over the prairie every year. "All the
cattle in the world seemed to be coming up from
Texas," one cowboy remembered.

A cattle drive could last over three months. The herds grazed along the way, so they would stay fat and sell for a good price. Ten or fifteen men could control two thousand or more cattle, moving about ten miles a day. The group included the trail boss and the wrangler, who took care of the horses. With them traveled a cook in a chuck wagon that was loaded with supplies. The cook, called cookie, was a very important man. He carried tools and sewing supplies, and acted as doctor. His wagon was the social center where everyone gathered to relax.

A CHUCK WAGON

His most important job was serving up three hot meals every day. He might make sourdough bread, biscuits and beans, potatoes, stew, or pie from dried fruit. Coffee had to be ready all the time. The first pre-roasted coffee beans were invented to fill the need for coffee that was easy to make anywhere—even on cattle drives.

Every package was sold with a stick of peppermint candy. The cook would use the candy to bribe one of the cowboys to grind the coffee beans for him. Good coffee was called "six shooter" because it was supposed to be so strong, a gun would float on it. Bad coffee was "coffin varnish."

Sitting around the fire at night, the cowboys would sing. Some of their songs were very rude. But others were sad. The most popular was called "Bury Me Not on the Lonesome Prairie." It told about a young dying cowboy who wanted to be buried back home. He was buried on the prairie anyway, and whenever cowboys passed his grave, they threw flowers.

At night, two men who stood guard sang to the cattle. They thought this helped keep the herd calm. If the cattle panicked, they would stampede. Anything unexpected, like a dropped cooking pot, or thunder, might set them off. Then the herd raced away in a wild mob. To stop them, the cowboys tried to make the cattle run in a circle. As the circle got tighter and tighter, they ran themselves to a standstill. During a stampede, it was easy for a

horse to trip or step in a gopher hole. If a cowboy was thrown from the saddle, he might be dragged or trampled to death by his horse.

Books and movies about the Wild West often show fights between cowboys and Indians. But in real life, they were rare. Cattle drives stayed on well-known trails. They did not go through hostile Indian territory. Usually the Indians were expecting them, and just charged a fee for the herds to cross their land.

Cowboy Lingo

Cowboys had their own colorful slang for everything. We still use some of it today:

Bread wallet: stomach

Cow juice: milk

Frog strangler: heavy rain

Hold your horses: Be patient

Horse feathers: ridiculous.

Pull in your horns: Back off

Shoot your mouth off: talk nonsense

Tenderfoot, greenhorn, dude, mail-order cowboy: an inexperienced cowboy

Whistle berries: beans

CHAPTER 5
Shoot-Outs on the Prairie

Prairie towns where the cattle drives ended were very rough places. They were full of hustlers, gamblers, and prostitutes hoping to make money from the cowboys. In 1870, only five hundred people lived in Abilene, Kansas, but there were thirty-two saloons. With so many drunken strangers around, things sometimes got violent.

When people think of cowboys, they usually think of gunfights. Actually, many cowboys didn't even carry pistols. They were more likely to carry a long gun like a rifle so they could fend off  coyotes or rattlesnakes, or kill a sick steer. But for most of their work, they didn't need a gun. They were not known for being good shots.

It was illegal to carry guns into many western towns. The cowboys had to hand in their guns when they arrived and pick them up again when they left. They would often celebrate leaving town by shooting their guns into the air as they rode off. This was called "hurrahing the town."

Western towns were not lawless. People expected criminals to be arrested and tried. The town marshal and his deputies were responsible for keeping order. If they needed help, they could call on a sheriff, who worked for the whole county. If a town was too small to have its own judge, it waited for a circuit judge who rode from town to town holding trials. Criminals were supposed to be held in jail until then.

A CIRCUIT JUDGE

In movies, two gunmen are often shown facing off in the town's main street. The man who draws, aims, and shoots the most quickly wins. In real life, most shootings were sneak attacks, not duels. But a few real duels did happen. A famous one was fought in 1865, in Springfield, Missouri.

Wild Bill Hickok was a professional gambler.

WILD BILL HICKOK

During a poker game, a man named Dave Tutt grabbed Hickok's gold pocket watch. Tutt said that Hickok owed him for a gambling debt. He announced that he would wear the watch in public. Hickok answered that if Tutt did, he was a dead man. That evening, the two men met up. Both drew and shot at the same moment. Tutt missed, and Hickok's shot killed him.

Hickok was arrested and tried. But the jury decided it was a fair fight. He later worked as a sheriff and a marshal in several towns in Kansas. In 1876, Hickok was shot in the back while playing poker. The hand of cards he was holding is still known as the "dead man's hand."

The open range lasted only a few decades. The prairie seemed endless, but it was not. Settlers were beginning to claim land in what would become the midwestern states. They didn't want other people's cattle grazing on their land and eating their crops.

Farmers wanted to build fences to keep cattle off their land. Some ranch owners wanted to fence in the land their cattle grazed on so no one else could use it. But on the prairie, it was hard to find good material to build a fence. This changed in the late 1860s, when barbed wire was invented. It was light, cheap, and sharp.

The invention of barbed wire led to the fence-cutting wars of the 1880s. Some farmers built fences right across cattle trails. Ranchers fenced off areas of prairie stretching from horizon to horizon so only their own cattle could graze there. They didn't always own the land. But neither did anyone else.

Anti-fencers secretly cut through the barbed wire in the middle of the night. When ranchers lay in wait to stop them, deadly gunfights broke out. To defend his fences, one man planted bombs at the base of the posts. If someone tried to cut the barbed wire, the bombs would go off. The government sided with the fence builders and passed laws to protect the fences.

As more and more land was fenced off, wandering herds sometimes starved. Then came the terrible winter of 1886–87. It was so cold that millions of cattle on the open prairie died. Some froze to death, and some suffocated when their breath froze. Cattle owners lost most of their herds. That was the end of the open range. From then on, successful ranchers owned their land privately. They confined their cattle in fenced areas where cowboys could keep an eye on them.

As railroads lines reached more and more western towns, the herds of cattle didn't need to be driven so far in order to reach a place where the meat could be shipped east. Cattle drives grew shorter. The famous trips where cowboys drove herds through the lonesome prairie for months became a story of the past.

CHAPTER 6
The End of the Buffalo

Cattle now grazed where the buffalo had lived for centuries. As many as sixty million buffalo had once wandered over the prairie. The first European explorers saw herds that stretched farther than the eye could see. By 1894, only a few hundred were left. What killed off so many of the buffalo?

The cattle boom was one important reason. When cattle overgrazed the open prairie, and fences blocked off acres of land, it got much harder for buffalo to find food.

Many of the Plains tribes, including the Crow, Blackfoot, and Comanche, hunted buffalo. For centuries, the Indians hunted only as many buffalo as they needed. This was not enough to kill them off. But then the fur traders showed up. They paid the Indians to kill many more buffalo for their hides. Soon traders started killing buffalo themselves as well.

COMANCHE

CROW

BLACKFOOT

Meanwhile, railroad lines were stretching out farther and farther west. Once they reached into the Great Plains, the buffalo were doomed. Railroads advertised special buffalo-killing trips. The train would run alongside a buffalo herd. Then hunters inside the train would shoot as many as possible—just for fun. One man killed almost six thousand buffalo all by himself in two months.

The US government thought getting rid of the buffalo was a good idea. Without buffalo to hunt, there would be no way for the Indians to continue their way of life on the prairie. They'd have to move onto reservations and settle down in one place. The prairie could be turned into farmland. The government believed, in the words of an army colonel, "Every buffalo dead is an Indian gone."

By the beginning of the twentieth century, the buffalo were almost extinct. The last remaining herd lived in Yellowstone National Park. Finally the government acted to rescue what was left. It became illegal to kill any animal within the park. The last herd was able to survive and grow. The huge herds of the past will never return, but in our own time the buffalo have started to come back. Some farmers raise them for meat. Today there are about 200,000 buffalo. Of these, 4,200 live in the wild.

BUFFALO CAUSING A MODERN-DAY TRAFFIC JAM IN YELLOWSTONE

CHAPTER 7
Gold Fever and Boomtowns

In 1848, gold fever struck in the West. Gold was discovered at Sutter's Mill in California, setting off a mining frenzy. Thousands of men raced out west, hoping to get rich quick. In 1849, the wildest year of the gold rush, about eighty thousand hopeful miners made the journey. They were known as the forty-niners.

The California gold rush is the most famous because it was the first and the biggest. But in the following years there were similar mining rushes all over the dry, rocky lands of the West. The land sometimes belonged to Indians. But few people cared. The Black Hills of South Dakota are sacred to the Sioux and Cheyenne Indians.

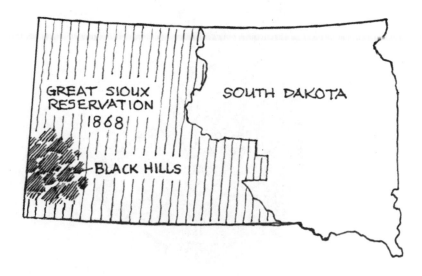

A treaty in 1868 with the US government promised the land to them forever. But when gold was found there, miners rushed in anyway.

An army officer named George Custer was sent to force the Indians out. The Indians fought back fiercely. After a series of bloody battles, Custer and all his men were killed at the Battle of the Little Bighorn, known as "Custer's Last Stand."

GEORGE CUSTER

Despite this victory, the Indians were driven out, and soon mines were being bored into the sacred Black Hills.

Mining towns sprang up almost overnight. They were known as boomtowns. At first the miners lived in tents. If the deposit (called a bonanza) was good enough for them to stay, they would build wooden shacks and a few businesses like a post office, a general store, or a hotel—and of course a few saloons.

Miners worked long, hard hours, with little time for anything else. Men usually came alone. They hoped to become rich, and then rejoin their families. A boomtown might have as many as nine men for every woman.

Mining towns were rough places. Robbery was a common crime. Gangs of robbers would lie in wait in a narrow pass to ambush a stagecoach or

wagon loaded with money and precious metals.

Stagecoaches carried armed guards, so robberies often turned into deadly gunfights. One famous stagecoach robber was "Black Bart." He dressed like a gentleman and treated his victims with great politeness. He sometimes left pieces of his own poetry at the scene of his crimes.

Other gangs would rob trains that carried gold. The most famous train robber was Jesse James. He sometimes loosened the rails of the track so that the train would derail. Then he went through the cars robbing passengers.

James and his gang also robbed banks. The gang sometimes committed robberies in broad daylight. They would show off in front of the admiring crowd before escaping.

Not only the trains were dangerous. So was the Pony Express.

The Pony Express

In 1860, the Pony Express was created to deliver the mail by fast horses. Some riders were as young as fourteen. They changed horses frequently, and at the end of his shift, a rider passed his bag to a new rider. Pony Express riders could deliver mail across the continent in ten days.

The Pony Express delivered mail out West. Riding for it was a risky job. Riders were sometimes targeted by thieves. And the route passed through the territory of the Paiute Indians, who were at war with the United States. The war prevented one Pony Express delivery from being made. This was the only time it ever failed to deliver the mail.

PONY EXPRESS BAG

In 1861, a telegraph line all the way to San Francisco was completed. Now news could travel to California instantly. This put the Pony Express out of business. The service has become a legendary part of the Wild West, but it actually lasted only nineteen months.

It was hard to keep law and order in mining towns. The county sheriff might be in another town and hard to reach. For day-to-day problems, people turned to the town marshal. Some town marshals were legendary. Willie Kennard of Yankee Hill, Colorado, was one of the West's few black marshals.

When he applied for the job, he was asked to prove himself. First he shot both guns out of the holsters of a murderer he was trying to arrest. Then

WILLIE KENNARD

he shot each of the man's two companions through the head before they could finish drawing on him. He arrested his man, made sure he had a legal trial, and hanged him. A man like this could keep order. But such men were rare. Many marshals actually worked *with* the criminals.

Sometimes gunfights between gangs and law officers broke out right in the middle of town. The best known of these is the shoot-out in 1881 near the O.K. Corral, in the silver-mining town of Tombstone, Arizona. It was between the Clanton-McLaury gang of cattle thieves and murderers, and Marshal Virgil Earp, his brothers Wyatt and Morgan, and their friend Doc Holliday, who were Virgil's deputies.

VIRGIL EARP   MORGAN EARP   WYATT EARP   DOC HOLLIDAY

At the time, it was just another shoot-out. But a biography of Wyatt Earp in 1931 and a 1957 movie called *Gunfight at the O.K. Corral* made it one of the most famous fights in the West.

Sometimes people took the law into their own hands. They believed it was easier to shoot someone than to wait for the slow action of the law. A whole town might be terrorized by a murderer or gang of robbers. Then the citizens would band together into a group called a posse. If they caught the criminals, they hanged them on the spot.

CHAPTER 8
Ghost Towns

If the mines prospered, the boomtown grew into a real town. People built churches, libraries, theaters, and schools. Some miners settled down and began to raise families. Their wives often ran boardinghouses for miners. They offered the men a clean bed and hot meals. Their children helped out with cooking, cleaning, serving, and laundry. When the boys were old enough, they would join their fathers working in the mines.

William Frederick "Buffalo Bill" Cody

Annie Oakley

Pony Express rider

Copy of the first letter carried by the Pony Express,
with news of Abraham Lincoln's election in 1860

Frontier hotel in California

Pioneers heading west to Nebraska, 1886

Daniel Boone

Cowboys driving cattle

A cowboy guards cattle in Arizona

A cowboy rounding up cattle in California

Underwood Archives/Getty Images

A bull rider hits the ground at a rodeo in Kansas City, Missouri

Cowboys on a long cattle drive from South Dakota to Nebraska

Cowboys at dinner

R.Y. Young/Hulton Archive/Getty Images

Staging of a typical saloon argument

Forty-niners looking for gold

1911 reenactment of a stage coach robbery

Jesse James

African American homesteaders in Nicodemus, Kansas

Sod house in Newell, South Dakota

Swazey Hotel in the ghost town of Bodie, California

A one-room schoolhouse on the prairie

Chinese laborers during the construction of the
Northern Pacific Railroad in Montana

Golden spike ceremony celebrating the completion of the transcontinental
railroad, Promontory Summit, Utah, May 10, 1869

Some boomtowns grew into cities such as Butte, Montana, that still survive today. Others disappeared as fast as they had arisen. If the vein of ore began to run out, people started to move away, until no one was left. The buildings were abandoned, and the town became a ghost town.

BUTTE, MONTANA, TODAY

Today, Bodie, California, is one of the best-preserved ghost towns. In 1879, it was home to around ten thousand people, with its own orchestra, three newspapers, a school, and sixty-five saloons. Three years later, the boom ended. Still, Bodie managed to survive as a small town until the 1930s, when a fire swept through. After that, only six people remained. Once they died, Bodie was left alone with its ghosts. The buildings are still full of furniture and personal belongings. In bedrooms, you can see fancy wallpaper peeling off the wall, and carved bedsteads. In the taverns, glasses and bottles still sit on the bar. Today Bodie is a state park open to the public.

BODIE, CALIFORNIA

CHAPTER 9
Stolen Lands

By the 1860s, the Great Plains were the only area of the United States that was inhabited mostly by the Indians. Congress decided it was time to take ownership of this last holdout. They wanted to divide the Great Plains into small farms owned by single families. In 1862, they passed the Homestead Act. This let anyone who was an American citizen—or wanted to become one—claim 160 acres of government land for only ten dollars. (Indians weren't included. They didn't become American citizens until 1924.) If the settlers built a house on the land and managed to farm for five years without starving, the property was theirs. The act didn't restrict who could claim land. A woman could do it, or an immigrant, or a black person.

One area of the prairie was not included in this act. A large piece of land covering part of what is now Oklahoma, Kansas, and Nebraska was officially Indian Territory. The government had forced many groups of Indians to live there, and promised they would keep it always.

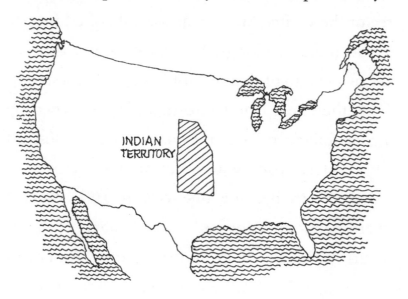

But soon settlers began to look at it greedily. In 1871, Congress passed the Dawes Act. This broke up Indian Territory into single plots. Any Indian who would accept a plot, farm it, and live like white people could do so and become an American citizen. Henry Dawes, who wrote the act, believed it would have a "civilizing effect on Indians because it forced them to cultivate land, live in European-inspired

HENRY DAWES

houses . . . [and] own property."

After each Indian was given his piece of land, the US government took back everything that was left over and sold it to white settlers. The Indians were given no choice. This was not a treaty to be discussed, agreed to, and signed. It was a law they had to obey. The act was a disaster for the Indians. Even those who tried to cooperate often lost their land. The Indians were supposed to keep the most fertile parts of their territory. But when it was divided up, they were often given the worst plots instead, where it was almost impossible to grow enough to survive. They got into debt and had to sell their plot. The Indians eventually lost almost two-thirds of the territory they had formerly been allowed to keep.

Some Plains Indians, especially the Dakota and Sioux, refused to accept the Dawes Act. They fought to keep their land. Bloody Indian wars broke out, lasting almost thirty years. Many people were killed on both sides, but in the end the Indians were beaten.

From the point of view of European settlers, the story of the Wild West was the story of "how the West was won." The settlers fought the Indian wars against "savages" who were trying to stop the march of civilization.

To the Indians it was another story entirely. The West was not "won," it was stolen. It was their home, and the settlers were cheating outsiders who broke every promise they made. The Indian

wars were fought by people desperate to protect
their tribal way of life from destruction. Anyone
who wants to understand the complete history
of the American West should seek out this other
story as well: not just how the West was won, but
how it was lost.

The Trail of Tears

The Cherokee, Chickasaw, Choctaw, Creek, and Seminole people were known as the "Five Civilized Nations." These Indians had originally lived in the East, where they had built farming villages that adopted many elements of the colonists' culture and blended them with their own traditions. However, the Indians' land was very fertile. Settlers wanted it. So in 1830, the tribes were driven off their farms and marched out to reservations in Indian Territory. The brutal march west, during which many Indians died, was known as "the Trail of Tears."

They were promised they would never be forced off their land again. Indian Territory would be theirs to keep "for as long as the grass grows and the waters run."

It did not take long for this promise to be broken.

CHAPTER 10
Homesteads

Before the Homestead Act, few people had wanted to settle on the prairie. But now that the land had been opened up, many changed their minds. As prairie towns grew, community leaders wanted to attract more people. They advertised to poor peasants in Europe. They described how much better life would be in the American West. Many European immigrants sailed across the Atlantic, got off the boat in New York City, and immediately headed out to Kansas, Wyoming, Colorado, or Dakota Territory.

People from the same country often found land to claim near one another. So towns sprang up that were entirely German, Swedish, or Norwegian. Often settlers continued to speak their own language and keep their old customs in the New World. People still cooked their traditional foods and celebrated their old holidays.

Some of the people who took advantage of the Homestead Act were former slaves. After the Civil War, they faced violence and discrimination in the South. Many had to work for their former masters in conditions that were not much better than slavery. Some black activists thought the best way former slaves could help themselves was to make a new start somewhere else. "Come West. . . . It is better to starve to death in Kansas than to be shot and killed in the South," one newspaper editorial urged.

Kansas was the most popular destination. In the years before the Civil War, every time a territory became a new state, people had fought over whether it would be a slave state or a free one. The battle in Kansas had been so fierce that people called it "bleeding Kansas." Now that the war was over, many blacks remembered how hard people in the state had fought to resist slavery. About fifteen thousand former slaves moved to

Kansas. Most traveled partway by boat along the Mississippi River. But some determined blacks who couldn't afford the fare walked all the way.

They called themselves Exodusters because they were moving to a free land, just as the Israelites had in the Bible, in their exodus from Egypt. Several groups founded all-black towns. The most successful of these communities was Nicodemus. The first settlers there were so poor, they couldn't afford farming equipment. But they survived. After other settlers joined them, they began to thrive. Soon there was a hotel, stores, schools, and churches. But when the train lines were extended out to Kansas, the railroads skipped Nicodemus. This was a big blow, and ended the town's growth. Still, Nicodemus never disappeared completely. Today it is a national historic landmark.

A FAMILY IN NICODEMUS

To anyone who had grown up with forests, the Great Plains was a shock. There were almost no trees, so it was impossible to build log cabins. People had to build out of what was there—dirt. For a quick shelter, they would dig into the side of a hill. This was called a dugout.

Or they could make a sod house or "soddy." The prairie sod was held together so tightly by grass roots that you could carve it up into bricks that

people jokingly called "Nebraska marble." A sod house had dirt floors and walls. People hung up sheets to keep dirt from dropping onto their heads. Some added wooden floors and wallpaper, to make it more homelike.

Families on prairie farms were often large. Any extra hands were a big help. Children worked alongside adults from a very early age. One Kansas farmer bragged that his two-year-old son could fetch the cows home from the fields, carry in wood for the stove, and feed the hogs all by himself.

Even in the smallest settlements, the children went to school for part of the year. When settlers arrived on the prairie, one of the first things they did was build a schoolhouse. These had only one

room. Children of all ages were taught by one teacher. Teachers could be as young as sixteen— no older than some of their students. Books and paper were expensive. So the children wrote on little handheld blackboards called slates. They shared their books. A popular schoolbook might be passed down from one generation to the next. Students studied spelling, reading, penmanship, grammar, arithmetic, and geography. Sometimes lessons were turned into a game. They might have spelling bees or race to see who could solve math problems in their heads more quickly.

The schools were strict. Students had to sit still and be quiet. They might be punished for making mistakes. But parts of school were fun. During the lunch break, they could go outside and play. This was the main chance they had to be with other kids outside their family.

CHAPTER 11
Proving a Claim

After settlers claimed a plot of land, they still had to earn the right to keep it. To "prove a claim" they had to live there for five years. The first years were especially difficult. Even though the land was cheap, it took money to get there. Supplies to plow and plant the soil were also expensive. And people needed enough to live on until they could harvest their first crop. Many had to borrow money in order to get started. Then they had a debt to pay off, on top of everything else.

Sometimes during the first years, a man had to leave the claim to find paying work elsewhere. But someone had to actually be living on the claimed land. So he would leave his wife and children behind.

Settlers arrived believing that the prairie soil was so fertile that life would be easy. One man wrote that every inch of his land was "as rich as cream." But people soon found out how hard it was to make a prairie farm pay. Frequent droughts led to bad harvests. Even worse were the plagues of grasshoppers. Thousands of insects would darken the sky, eating everything in their path. In a bad year, the streams would be clogged with the bodies of dead grasshoppers. Prairie fires were also a danger. On the flat, open grassland, a fire could race out of control for miles. People had to dig ditches around their house and fields to turn the fire aside.

A different kind of problem was loneliness. In Europe, peasants had lived in small, close-knit villages. But because of the way the Homestead Act was written, in the American West every family had to live on a separate piece of land. The nearest neighbor might be miles away.

People got together whenever they could. Like the log cabin pioneers, they turned work into a party. Neighbors would gather together for a barn raising, the harvest, or a quilting bee.

Still, a lot of time was spent alone on the empty prairie. It was worst in winter, when heavy snows made traveling difficult and dangerous. Settlers might go for months without seeing anyone beyond their own family.

Some people couldn't stand it. One magazine editor remarked, "An alarming amount of insanity occurs in the new prairie States among farmers and their wives." This was known as "prairie madness." Today we would call it depression. "I have nervous breakdown while baking pancakes last Saturday. In bed since," one woman wrote in her diary. Most people were able to recover. A few gave up.

Life was hard. But back East, most of the settlers could never have hoped to own their own farm. They would have spent their lives working for someone else. In the West, they were independent. "What a pleasure it is to work one's own farm," one man wrote after years of hardship, "for you can feel that it is yours and not for someone else."

CHAPTER 12
The Closing of the Frontier

Almost from the beginning of the movement west, the place where the frontier began was where the railroads stopped. For instance, the Oregon Trail started at the last point travelers could reach by train. And as settlers spread across the prairie and built towns, the train lines followed them.

In 1862, Congress passed the Pacific Railroad Act. A railroad would run all the way across the continent. Two companies were created to build the railroad. One started in the West and worked east; the other started in the East and worked west. Each raced to build faster than the other.

Much of the work was done by immigrants,

especially the Chinese and Irish. These men faced enormous hardships. They had to blast through mountains and lay track in deserts. Some of the railroad men became folk heroes. The most famous is John Henry, the "steel driving man." He was a black workman whose job was to drive a steel drill into rock. He raced against a steam-powered drill and won, but died in the effort.

In 1869, the two halves of the railroad were joined together in Promontory Summit, Utah. The trip from the Atlantic to the Pacific had once taken pioneers on the Oregon Trail six rough and dangerous months. Now it could be done in comfort in only eight days. The entire continent was linked by modern technology.

Twenty-one years later, in 1890, the government announced that the western frontier no longer existed. Settlers had spread over the entire continent from coast to coast. The Wild West was coming to an end.

Timeline of the Wild West

1763 — British government promises Indians all land west of the Appalachian Mountains

1785 — US government divides land along Ohio River and sells it to settlers

1830 — The Five Civilized Nations are forced west on the Trail of Tears

1843 — The Great Migration

1848 — Gold discovered at Sutter's Mill

1860 — Pony Express created

1861 — Telegraph line to San Francisco completed; the Pony Express goes out of business

1862 — Congress passes the Homestead Act and the Pacific Railroad Act

1868 — Treaty promises the Black Hills of South Dakota to the Sioux and Cheyenne Indians

1869 — Two halves of the Transcontinental Railroad are joined together

1871 — Dawes Act is passed

1876 — Battle of the Little Bighorn, Custer's Last Stand

1881 — Shoot-out near the O.K. Corral

1886 — Severe winter causes millions of cattle to die out on the prairie

1890 — US government announces that the western frontier no longer exists

Timeline of the World

1704 — French and Indians massacre English settlers at Deerfield, Massachusetts

1707 — United Kingdom of Great Britain formed from England, Scotland, and Wales

1773 — The Boston Tea Party

1789 — French Revolution begins

1839 — First Opium War between Britain and China

1848 — Karl Marx and Friedrich Engels publish *The Communist Manifesto*

1854 — Florence Nightingale begins to nurse wounded British soldiers in the Crimea

1861 — US Civil War begins

1867 — Shogun rule ends in Japan

1869 — Suez Canal opens

1876 — Alexander Graham Bell patents the telephone

1877 — Tchaikovsky's ballet *Swan Lake* premieres in Moscow

1882 — Standard Oil Trust becomes the first industrial monopoly

1889 — Eiffel Tower is completed

1895 — X-rays discovered

1904 — New York City subway opens

Bibliography

*Books for young readers

*Freedman, Russell. *Children of the Wild West*. New York: Clarion Books, 1983.

Hine, Robert V., and John Mack Faragher. *Frontiers: A Short History of the American West*. Lamar Series in Western History. New Haven, CT: Yale University Press, 2007.

Milner, Clyde A., Carol A. O'Connor, and Martha A. Sandweiss, eds. *The Oxford History of the American West*. New York: Oxford University Press, 1994.

*Ward, Geoffrey C. Preface by Stephen Ives and Ken Burns. *The West: An Illustrated History*. Boston: Little, Brown, 1996.

WEBSITES

Legends of America. Old West Legends: Adventures in the American West
www.legendsofamerica.com/oldwest.html

The Wild West
www.thewildwest.org